Midway Radicals & Archi-Poems

Midway Radicals & Archi-Poems

TED LANDRUM

Garry Thomas Morse, Editor

Signature EDITIONS

Cover design by Doowah Design.
Cover image: "1234 House_02" by Lars Lerup, 1985. Private Collection, courtesy Betts Project.
Photo of Ted Landrum by Lisa Landrum.

This book was printed on Ancient Forest Friendly paper.
Printed and bound in Canada by Hignell Book Printing Inc.

We acknowledge the support of The Canada Council for the Arts and the Manitoba Arts Council for our publishing program.

Library and Archives Canada Cataloguing in Publication

Landrum, Ted, 1968–, author
Midway radicals & archi-poems / Ted Landrum.

Poems.
ISBN 978-1-77324-004-6 (softcover)

I. Title.

PS8623.A5138M53 2017 C811'.6 C2017-901417-X

Signature Editions
P.O. Box 206, RPO Corydon, Winnipeg, Manitoba, R3M 3S7
www.signature-editions.com

Be radical—be radical—be not too damned radical!

Walt Whitman

In the middle—there is the place of the poem.

Paul Celan

Cutting through the middle—we encounter ideas.
This makes all the difference in inquiries.

Plato

Contents

Agog	**9**
How Speak	**10**
Sticks & Stones, a reWorlding	**12**
Inauguries	**13**
Fly-Trap Test	**16**
So Nets a beginning	**17**
Aristotle's Nik, fragments	**18**
Art History (with Hiccups)	**22**
Roland the Para-Tower	**23**
Ark Fundations, Roving Renovations (8 beams)	**24**
Orgy of Cities	**28**
Time Materials	**29**
Age of Huts, Midway Para-Cuts	**30**
Halfabet: words leaping Manifest No	**38**
Tunnelling Through	**39**
Xeno Laps	**40**
Writing an aid to me	**44**
Odyssey Poem	**60**
Measure	**61**
Hunt for Optimism in the Middle Bridged	**62**

So Nets the middle of Crosby and Bleecker **70**
Last words from Creeley, a gain **71**
Human Universe **72**
Twombly > Chicago > NY **76**
Language & Architecture **77**
WORDpark **78**
Arch of Enjoyment **79**
Systematic Encounter (in Plural Parts): The Plan, revised for Epimetheus; Hephaestean Paradigm, with Off-Cut Frivolities for Understudy Mask Distribution; and, Snippets of Kairos for Enkidu Haircut **86**
Hephaestus, laughed at by gods **89**
Poe—inciples Concentrate **90**
Lamp of Beauty **92**
If Tower **95**
Roland's Tower, X'd **96**

Notes on Poems & Sources **101**
Acknowledgements **104**
About the Author **105**

Agog

the poet hammers up
to demand
the right
light
to exhume
the lost will
of us
every word
ours for life
listens in the cells

HOW SPEAK so as to *stir*

so as it
were

influential qualitative *w i n d s* ?

how s a y so as to blow away

proud airs of fettered prudence ?

with what words
would one s w a y
uttermost yoke and reins reluctant to our
founding
wish
& Will
for
fond
freshening

Well

Let us FIND
and / or fix them NOT in large lucid languages

clear of *wondering*

THIS

Rather Ring
our vow levered CANT

past jargon's lists hisss howl yawn kiss

fling far
our worry wardy fare

fetch near *foundling miraculousness*

pause and breathe

pleas in the making
TAKE up
AWAKENING

Mouths Eyes Hands Ears

OPEN WIDE

each least *BECKONING'S* re markable degree:

Hmnmnm paiax!
whhOOAw PApai! pa

Collooh *YAWP* Callay
OIMOI *Otototoi Popoi*
euuuuu-eu EUIOUpia
O! Moly
O? You tOOOOpia a *aaaaahh*
Hoi Poloi pia : Whrrwhee!
HA! hee *eh?*

O[a]**R** swear momentous
hEUREKAStyx
! in the intercoastal tub and liquid reckoning
of open minds'
mosaic depths

OR[e] risk inventing:
hHh! conflating inwyrd sup with 'magination's
r elations
resuscitating KIND of surprising in spy

Ur *Gwion* goin' *bach* to baby-lib Taliesin's
corner haunting
mortal muting charmmmm:

blerwm blerwm blerwm blerwm blerwm

blerwm blerwm blerwm blerwm

Otherwise sway by *placing*
moot
amble queries
sounding schemas
probing stances
in the manner of *pensive persons* composing motley MOTIVES

How else host well-meaning's wink

to kindle *Qualia* and MAKE
un sink

Our tangled *gist* and *spark*
Our SUSPECT
SITUATION

Sticks & Stones, a reWorlding

sticks & stones
build moments
of energy war
test
lockwork
in lines

begun
as art

hard work
knowing each move
unmoves
closer

you & you
tether
half way
to ending
room
to meet
each end

Inauguries

before as again
primordial latent *qualia* gurgle
in bowls and shoals of *populus*
potent tracings burgle forth
quasi-cusps and crave
as vexing myths froth worth
coiling diurnals ripple and surge
all else dormant curiosity
save these rare anticipant dribs

free-willed animas gather round
qua expectant earthen earhooks
lap loosing scrap sound shares
whole as kindled kinds can fête
peculiar portioned feats

simply put:
as phanta-plasmic-organo-flits
fit about worlds of interest
nearly made articulable
ephemeral generations crop themselves
on breach of memory
wild popular ever flattening gob
gone fundamental fragmentary same

again as before
early fabulous features
roily boily already burble
over

under spheral plenum's porous crock
percolating effervescent flitch and swale
recarbonated mucky-muck ripe with perturbation
fecund as permeable to flim-flam-flocculus
resampling candy fathomed core
as quintessential slurry treats splice and store
capabilities amply steepening

            simply put:
before one is in on quality's foil filigree
one has yet to put upon flesh
persnickety thresh of casual devisings
soon is soon enough to stress
this chastening storm nevertheless
behind beneath its building
plausibility's curtain
                                    weird uncertain

            forthwith
rhythmic haste must get on in with
                                                            if

wherein thereafter hence thence whence
whether will can find if's nipple mouth
or know now how we root about
forming reforming discontents

            which is to say:
                                                  surprise
enough to field spontaneous
                                                  arrivals

as turtled anticipation defends fresh findings
rehearse transmissive potentencies and linger
in nested tests of toiling temper-tude
whoever found best what least tempted
latent publics pending seedlings gone genera
vaulting knot-laced traps of mutual premonition
back against the storied nut of wall
as vital fade and tidal verge do rival
harboured feelings' splendid draw and splurge
on fancies taken in a curb

moreover
truth's backdoor knock schemata
need pit against power's
see-through palace of fit occasions
plying thresholds of pluripotent sense
here too we now merge on these
qualified ballistic spore criteria

(as far as willing interests
invest at all in fulcrum arts of causal being
or gravitate to keenest tilting
kind of ludic disposition)

again as before
advance a figure
reopening further if stranger means
choice change's active in-betweens
profuse peculiar mingle-hastening songs
fortuitous thwarts and throngs
intractable as danger
to the free

Fly-Trap Test

thinking a thought
(deep or not)
if at all a thought
worthy of daring
worthy of sharing
take this thought
(whatever it is)
and lay it up
against the
fly-trap
test
*

you know the one
old whispering yellowy guardian tongue
formerly found false flowering
mid open window minds
now curling in
now again out
captivated
captivating
slender twist of sap
subject to listing tryst of breeze
'til fleeting figures
(aeolian or aleatoric)
begin again to light
in and out of day
in and out of night
being a bit backlit
agog! *anon*? strange but familiar sight
some struggling still plays on
upon this long embattled sill
busy wriggling agon-buzz
(whether at war or peace)

jeeez! *please*

when thinking a thought
if at all a thought
worthy of snaring
worthy of bearing
we owe the gist of it
to pester mortal thought
give it a try !
how far can it fly
will it soon land
how close will it lie
how long
will it
stick
?

So Nets a beginning

piercing some point   corners have presence
warmth in the room structured dance
architect, weave among portent
fragments of fragments

hello earbook   running   in the streets
inhabit the day marvels
sunbody notebook
late to my hands

strong song in sail   an evening bristling
eyelids of thought   bathing in shadow
flows can pass by burst sea
all knees wanly

time spoke to our feetbridge
old long trail   thinks   cities gather
led on like sky
every handstand gives

occasion forge once went like night wrench
matter parade   on currents   rare to know
names like a year   ear
pure sense   and a day

...

ur spore   sent air moves   lightly
but strength nestled again   over jump haste of thought
bring on the windmind
turning light
fading tracks

Aristotle's Nik, fragments

— 3 —

some starting point   which presupposes
therefore proceeds   which is therefore
by then   a state of demonstrate
and has the other   in a certain way
that
not better known to knowledge
only then be taken as how to make

both making and acting   are
the discussions outside our school

state of capacity
the not included   is   acting making
since architecture is an art of capacity to make
such a state   an art-art   is identical
involving a true course coming into being
and considering how
is capable

whose origin is in the maker   and not
neither by necessity nor in accordance with nature
since
making and acting   must be a matter of
sense-objects
as chance loves

— 8 —

the man deliberating is aiming in
accordance with things attainable

concerned with universals also
recognize concerned particulars

especially those others who know
knew lights are digestible
but did not know health   whole health

concerned with
should have both forms to the former

but here
kind relations between wisdom and practical
their essence   concerned the city   plays
an *architectonic* part
related to the general to do with action
to be carried out in the act
this is why to *take part in politics*
for things as do things
also is concerned with
this is known
of the other another
and of the other
judicial

— 11 —

but again
excellence involves thinking while

even the stage does so
searching for something and is
hence
we must first inquire what it is about

plainly excellence is not any and every clever

a result of will a great good thing of
that which tends to attain

what one ought to do
means the middle too
is not yet excellence
in which one attains what again is
while another in the former excellence

in regard to
the end the manner and the time

to have deliberated well
with reference to what is

— 15 —

it would be thought strange
if
being over it
the *archi-poetry* which orders it
questions the difficulties first

let us say that
in choice of the two neither produces
they do produce health   however

so does being a part of
being possessed by
happy work

practical wiz makes us aim
at the right mark take the right means

Art History (with Hiccups)

after Lydia Davis, Pliny & Aristophanes

Modelled by the long b–~–*urning* light
of a tragic evening sun –~– the first drawing
a modest work of art made for no b–~–*uyer*
was traced by a young bride to be named
Pandora the adopted daugh–~–*ter*
of a maker of lucrative but fragile
and rudimentary clay jars
She did so upon learning suddenly
in the midst of an inter–~–*rupted* prenuptial meal
that her young lover being both obliged and ea–~–*ger* to test his manhood
must leave their camp before nightfall –~– He had been called a–~–*way*
(by rival suitors perhaps) to fight a distant bloody war –~– or else to s–~–*lay*
some ferocious beast plaguing probably inde–~–*fensible* borders of collective imagination
Fearing he might not return –~– Pandora contrived to cast their em–~–*bracing* shadows
onto the smooth cleft face of a large fallen rock –~– happily –~– within arms r–~–*each*
So near to them was it moreover that this very fallen rock –~–prior to their interruption
had made –~– their romantic d–~–*inner* fire –~– a private one
With the charred tip of a roasting st–~–*ick* still dripping with succulent juices
the pair made quick art together –~– (in collaboration with the setting s–~–*un*)
by tracing the poignant outline of their doubled –~– and doubly ab–~–*sent* shadows
Against this fractured stone then a charming and somewhat mysteriously rounded figure
their b–~–*ig* shadow-drawing made –~– capturing as it did their twin arched backs
with four arms –~– and four legs –~– and a b–~–*eastly* two-faced head
his face over her body hers over his facing opposite directions in space and time
Meanwhile –~– in the midst of their f–~–*air* coupled form
a lick of flickering firelight –~– melted and welded
whatever subtle differences came between them
in this an–~–*xious* moment of
interrupted love

Roland the Para-Tower

Ma
the tower is friendly
the tower is
earth and even

this virtually empty
tower
in order to satisfy
borders irrational

this double move
a movie
we visit

leaning
the tower looks it
into space

one might say
co-telligent forms
like *eu-Jour*
—opening well—
decipherment

what in fact is
mind before image
this ally
architecture

once these points
initiate
contemplate
an or stance
in order to stand

contrary reality
towers over
a world

Ark Fundations, Roving Renovations (8 beams)

§

elect
fifty
zig-zag
corona
tive
flicker
knocks
circumambi
lanced
on a
caged
hat
i
tip
Mid
alt.
glued
in a
loud
act

§

arkling
fiddling
ruffle
up
era
whisk
in
ornamentation
lilt
lucid
quill in a
win
tri
staccato
cluster
be in time
art

§

play of space
air
screen
re
settles
age of para
separa
pen and
wall
elastic
slow moti
un
going
between
in
yes
on so
suddenly reversing
now is the front

§

know
dawn the re
quickening
of
make
amidst
a
plete
bent
in the centre
edge
in
fie
pro
amaze
can
see
cry
i
us

§

do as a
ride
act
circling
up the slide
garden of
ties
pre
spectacle
muse
hero
sense
a
knock
again
on
stars
jam
a delicate hammer
i
carry
on
jets
din a
rally
for
fast
dance archi
time

§

on
will
resilience
re we
or we re
mingle
celebra
para
lex
sing from
vast
go far
gain
ody
chroma
is
un
rot
in
ear garden
world begins
rough
galaxa
nating
posi
arc
co
archies of
adagio

§

of a wind
know a
questioned
answer
as if
two
portions
now
one pattern
pace
everywhere
here
to leaf the now
much
faster
sun
shadows
suspended
image
our compass
vortex
midpath
para
can pulsate
the roots of
i

§

re
do
undinga
ur
lack
a gain
err
i
let
the here
light
orb
wide
a be
into
still as
air
re
the foundations

Orgy of Cities

dancing action reanimates walls
draws to send a figure of the ways
a figure ventures

imagining news
the young come dreaming
draw to make clever
plying new/old city collages

time's great ark an ear in moonlight

what's left of love's make
among amusements

pleasant labours

wine craft gold
kept care
returns

Time Materials

layers   we err   win on
un-light   in   or bodies
cold curry   inking down
all this poem is   not to re-port
a theft of   word position

o   fess the is-tort
pst   at thine art
ur to go on painting
gets to be   rad

to rend   horizons
sense   gist
then rip   if   a door

Age of Huts, Midway Para-Cuts

wayward   we planet
each   a dog
       chest conditions
       a single word
my mother moment
will it   become one language
question
i rent   sentence
this is urban planning
this is not   i wrote it
another story to smoke cigars
what of it

survive rose and red
       legal medicine
       law that tradition proposed
is wit   formal possibility systems
if this   were now it
everything here
i chose   vocabulary
because re pre sent a t ion
perhaps poetry can poem in a poem

page seems as a boy
rid of   verbalivity
if the pen won't if
how can   identical
ana-draw a floor map

our existence is the meaning of this
work as students knew
what writing meant

mad remain how is something
it doesn't   inherently possess

term in me   closer
would
the man hat   happen to Hitler a friend

record truth   speech itself
confused   poets
what an onion
does fit   poetry behavior
the answer   to question

win sons   what any of us even is
speech speaker analog
in such fiction   ratio
poets paradigm the word world

formal petition
hope language as a medium
attracts thought
could make the age disappear
everything this is
ugliness active
time   the muscle

etymology assumption
which is not true
is   if   it did increase
limits
the pre sum way wit hit
as eco book   he's content
to mean   what i like

magic   is a certain term
poetry   a state of view
the very idea   not the case
why   is the conception

suppose i was trying
native tongue
sand poetry
under these conditions
by the very act of the case
i have choice
there is also sleep
this cunning an offshoot, etc.
ant success a social definitope
of the whole
if
bores leave what happened
to rent
if i am crossing the alps
the poem requires the decision
or not to follow
is art of the process
i am continually written
what if states of mind
alter this operation

certainly given to design
sentence one can position abstract act
directly
impossible ions
story of a chimpbird
carried the force of prophecy

any term now greater than a place
language
what do nouns real the idea of
that perhaps
a demic one a-specialized readers

what makes exists on
or existed

i want the spaces poems leave

        the as perception

go make such a distinct i

on those who miss the point when i rove

this statement before everything else

the syntax   the order of this room

ate   put myself on

change time is my concept sentence

subjects age so time the flaw for the page

        when i was you

net of rules by which it is

processed   bets of rules

compare   s and 3

        i and not one

right   a hill with two peaks

prior to language than argument

Paris is in Paris

the question within the quest

references   i like it

on leaning less

poems   construct distance

work   a distant word

        can describe

a curve the sun knows

what we meant thereby

        ceded all assumptions

        the historical pens

if you redefine language

content   is only a nose

        of words

if one denies   now
this post-synactical implodes
terms
the miniaturist sets in abstract
art to move   Steve Reich

the concept   a list
imperialism
if poetry cannot be perfect
i began writing
i am the possible
conclusions   why is a poem

one be but leaving out
it is   our interpretation
of air
makes the referential
there
a rewrite   arks
also pre   sent on
paging a bout
perception   language

the present   a t
i on a lism
k on to work
what is it   allows sky
literary criticism
but is it   distortion of distortions

can one even say individual words
possibly   if
one approached
the inclusion of this

but how   if
has written no poems
per se
per form
as is   the fact of
film   wake judgments

what if i   told told you
periodic ally positions
i find   applicable
to all
if   at this point i was
to insert   change

lip is no tit   becomes
us language
if i could make a nurse
i would

what you re read
make   a note
in some other
note
i want form   to rain at will
form that is   actedness

a writ rest for this fact
a lone word   is commerce
one type   a judgment
its intention
butter's original intention
perhaps this poem
could be said
to bed
71 is distinctions
re ifications   pre sent
a poem in pencil

when i was you
                    the age
deliberate   deter
                    mining what will be written
if i we   re position

how far   will a term
                    mean
possibly   tic
if one could   be the poem
or could one   hive examples

why is an or   language context
                    against the ally

be re petition   a lit son

                    blow poetry
not necessarily poems

i sly   does it try
as   before
but   words
they are   a friend
a member of thunder
                    stand
                    de mining
                    each born tradition
a positive   i imagine
any language   on walls still apt to do
                    this
                    this tone
                    this train
imagine   omen
here   chased

running through fun
faster
the form   a hidden presence
                  and or dimension
a re me   or different

a paper pieces
                  words
to lip   any what
                  any one does
the day i room
                  is

whether one sees language
                  as era
rent in form   new things appear

values are a language
                  various as any

like eyes   i expect
                  i do
in the act of
reading   the ocean's ocean

building just   is a proof
why me   an ification of

its poemhood   lands

                  This
                  i sit

Halfabet: words leaping Manifest No

curious
a new theatre
to old forms
work in
and involuntary play
Between architecture

Tunnelling Through

	undermines	the runaround
	shortcuts	superficial
Tunnelling through	wins	the race the tortoise and the hare
	maps	fallacies of Zeno
	plants	fortuity and *loot*
Tunnelling through	heaves-up	ego-shed sarcophagi
	reaps	utilities certain worlds forgot
	slips-into	what we never knew we knew
Tunnelling through	stores	chores that yet may stir long lain masses
	speeds	what firm roots seek
Tunnelling through	finds	equivocal-antinomy-forks matriculate
	faces-down	purple's red orange's yellow green's blue
Tunnelling through	disappears	while others (waiting) melt
	catches	time below its belt
Tunnelling through	channels	wilderness
	smuggles	Buddha dreams
	stretches	latent limits of categorical truth
Tunnelling through	remembers	what weather means for Zeus
Tunnelling through	cuts	all sames
	zones	differences too (inner and outer)
	digs	pleasure-measuring diversity shares
Tunnelling through	tempers	what is new
	pacifies	instantaneity
	loosens	the bowels of history
	flushes	demagoguery poop
Tunnelling through	drains	logic shaken through a sieve
	tickles	the ramparts of antipathy and fear
	tames	volcanic arts in advance of mortal fire
Tunnelling through	cultivates	micromagnanimities
	picks	petty lockets' infra-cagey turf war zoos
Tunnelling through	mingles	our lingering bones
	humbles	eternity
	connects	finite me to improbable infinite *you*

Xeno Laps

sibyl	a mighty
drome	knower of
us	a
glad	tune
as a cup	rain
flames	to pry
off	or
on	if
wells	and
churns	will
led by teams	wish to
carry	let me hide the
ship	here

§

form	tempest found
us	a harbour
a remake	seeking
our writ in	no asylum
seeing	the hunt
burst into	a void
scaping	re
go transmutations	hiding
angle	for the
is shape	which
is ness	must de
malice	a
child	Proteus
born	to search

the whim trickery by
ray or
line here turns
on what who
on some rock into
whenlight now
all for
the wolf that
leaps to have
jubilance murmur
on as
not forgotten con
thin as
a mist is voice

§

sublime ur soothed by
lighting the rad led
us in
again then
rid of
the it
re unbeknownst here co
add read arch
to be a song an
aid spoke
into depths
the heights of old
self rising like a
trace after scatter

gather promise
as tinsel
fate's ear over
lack like
sand might give
the river a threshold
in the house of us less is
just war to
the furies that
dog the
wheel hence caves
tell us
heat, bring a
warm self to sleep

§

stretch our
thin nest
in the drift edge
ages sole night
ying ring
ferryman to
pass like us
twice wandering art
cleave the if
geo on the
rift a
steep all is or
river ing the
sighs carve a part

the fields’ ailments hath
no rest ’cause the
us hat danced
in the eddies see
worn ur before
us giving
shore seeing
a god surrender
dream locks
in a
spool then up
vanishes shines a goddess
on off
a re leaving touched

§

mornings writing
us bouquets here we
let in a loud
fling to assemble
laugh nice clinging on the
rove within my
other heart
shrines of
pulls beyond the
yoke conquered
sting leaves me
the flow of
air toying with the geo
a strange port dreaming us

Writing an aid to me

moon press arts blished in paper portions
pre wish an operation found
oration bells to graphalog an aid to me

un states of un
re trans co written
within the make we ourselves make it
if with our sound

soft occasion felt disquiet
sed to me
raw hope is certainty lopping off the limit

forged memory is girth press say power
to say if
rent parts of ody elements
petition air a flesh in great versatility
ends the middle reopened now
a science continuous
for it is possible to carry the impossible
influence action beyond the if
true beauty indispensible to the smallest human bones

unknown pressed with questions
incessant complexity's entire face here
sorrow desire impossible to pull to
put to attention
the whole room cut to come to
people made by language

writing an aid to me
i know around saying
a hundred errors
sure up the arts of life

here a bridge of name painting
the human back of trees
a living wedge saw time is architect
thin as a rest can visit
now problems
a point of increasing we
with simple verse

us a few hoops up
row the familiar side of how
did this begin a *gr* party
charm hacking a do music

direct time is our swell alt.
the ific we taste of a mixed trace
as a spring beat we clink
a group of be and
cast further care in a heck
make it promise
dreams of ally in a look

up between us and up is us joined
to draw a link ink in one act
let to its geo life stance
laden with later portion

considerable script the readymade
sent time reading
up bristling with ink fuss
so yell grand the poor scratch
spent in the able
hone able us the verybody
in a link all here ink

as i sort to mark nice arches
out sun similar to the better shining
out *yup* a like link of choice distance
tremble the word branch
in the under they eddy

un bag the middle
print fire flying in memory paint
at night darling giant
lop the action of look envelopes
a large row brief in the *ugh* dawn
meaning puff of reason to the push of reaches
between secret ears with ur
this flesh tree under the window
ear vine learning to make us use the fable

each imagine a full see mind to glass the whole
sated among pearls landing in speech

to seek another go
round speech anima
re re ruse un door fragments with a deep repeat it

or
trying in detail dire self can attract a tiny syllable
is
the beginning of the other a struggle in the same
two forth this is love the live ear

memory paint means action out of abstraction
in the way order roughly
for small makes fix full quire as far
or
pile five deep in children of flexible thought

show your muse graphical work and move the parted
past formation to passion tones
order forge the pal source
ate rough a language music of changes
new *ish* for know the road in motion

sed student well being is
hook into tug what else but time
reading in patches
be hook is hop all
when going so made talk enjoyment
tend the ground
shook
think range
go pen in the act place
ration of love in step
lift off in act
under the be stands

slow pinch art bends the sky under onward
face that face as names in ink
touch on time's play work
trying to get beneath is hilarious
so may distance bump the usual for ideas
a sting flow heads to zero

plumb this much
feet the floor is early
touch is the other
so i on layers nail crow work
round as the instant rolls over whole
bent low by the great ying
way enters
building the joiners

the term work is pitch beautiful
link to many choices
say time wind water plural the curious

to pen hidden human a building
ask as mediate measure to imagine other
semble motions of us thought
keeping with time keen on difficulty
on every time edge is doing

ur ally our town torn
scribes interruption
read and fly that red ink as we ink
revise roots and love the found laugh

as ideas pass ably between points
meeting ambling methods
no hope indicates a finish
there is only a riddle
and gossip falls fast
while power words toward thought
face of the world its way fine
to live fully otherwise
remind me otherwise

one ark re posits the world
beginning with intention's retro prospective
illusion of if sequences us chance can imagine
words make ions utter
far comes to term

struggle the plural as full convictions
the arbitrary world responds here
is shed form bound as tight work
by the time press

arch language rain
as
the possibility of signification
returns outward ally
life
lifted in the if
a laugh cure rightly flies
the wild flow
lifted wonderment

dull buzz woke the blue face in open being
working the dire day work of knowing to roll over

a good roll the reverse
plans a natural confusion
an occasion more able to utter in minute ink wishes
in patterns of time
the invented i you me
turn
a little if only
in only love a love is sage

the law of scenes by colours mean
reality rolling on as is

us contrast as space language
fold between the formwork
a tender beauty
we the animals please
for half change is reaching

petition the opening occurring in colour
a room you'll pace
the choice links hone in on thought
for part other
for memory wall beneath art
legible pace startling doors of notice
in art of the found ask
an us space
read

ask beyond the scrap of bits
to see world thought hop the real
easy to ask
sly around touch on ur
be finds middle in kind
the lean if
is fit on a place to scribble

Thursday sent silk back
for methods are a long scribe
the hand is in the re on wows
other ear spin made the win war on
so say tickle now might more confess
more nature of shed sequel
carries more the ear force

the eye is made talk over
in the rent place by a flow great
in my own eye clumsy diction soaring clear
obviously wrong or beautiful play

one city is a variety of tripartite us superstition
dia co loom health to the melody things
some read as a kind of city
and do out of the riddle
other better borders
any limit fixing beauty daily
every blind fuddle the bar
some us aid of recall
in books erasing a limit

do know a town landed
act that range a little distance
to each is filled with ink
its little place hopes double up
sent help tends a re member

here is putty say rolling for beauty
touch and time trick invisibly us
and possibly please

a name could bend uncertainty with a trick well done
mind watching a world back you
if stuck middle deliberate on a nervous re thing
its little place is total ally
book for good sharp if arts
a little confusion introduces lack
turns dazzling in the us pace of existence disco
ur space the happiness of rhythm words
the order in history

the flying head a seedy core
rose as ark of understanding finite fictions
a small wonder moves the whole rather careful
throwing discovery some proper affection
mate diving on level ruins moved in the wine

body praises everyone
and should be if even a close order
to begin art as the other find much in the ground preceding re paces
ear drawing to buzz songs

link large in the other
is an ordinary way to be acquainted with might
between each round of thing thought
no name usage houses character
petition writing constitutes the mind in the mind

very many touch at able ears
do love a digression rove
little ink wrinkle
one mode not standing united in memory
raise we mutter like an arch of many worlds

beauty is its past led up laughing to be passion
re judgments apt art to frame a play
understanding latent
trying occupies at bottom
makes a little aim of making
act
mean to make a show
link
by means the sun does not exclude

love the best scuttle
sembling course art of all sizes
being danger dense in rig distance
fit distance apter by writing made real

pen an activity
do ear a melody
be so and so in relations written as so and so

log us
inkulate letters as ardors and ear pathos
as house ears made ages grow jectures

us reading the day rules
ample able above the roof
as play does per minute
a week a year clear of
can't you sort of lie a spark ark yes in my ear art
no win rooms that irony a little fun window
each play solo-selves another
dub in knowing now more of it
for a long art may perfect inking with others

utter ear a mud binder
mixing with a lit mix of do if as
into time art

swing in the fore source draws
ink gest as waters fringe
qua into arked page
beauty's comfort traffic
story work us-fulness
to the side of dual excitement

trip at the words
ink it in hitch locks just
fine remains ambiguous
ses *ish* it just
include the original ire

click in half a re wild loop
loose like a bond in public
doing rites of in which

sing on is a wall you keep
and the little window an infinite image
between the background mess
same variation without limit
body finite turns in theory
the bridge gap in risk

like a self or not
speaking a through twinkle
a city body by love philosophy

copy's word farm
name work settled the country
over a mile of paper
a poem
no such thing put in a bank
pen humans can circle as common mates
speak to the house we re raise
like things re found re cast

many may rent rock bottom a high trade
almost to the rescue
a happy little say door
being key change for the occasion
sent on punctuation formation
fuses sweeter in the grip

ur legend is dual
the arch pen life here
or fig script window
all scope in era
flowers forth a co scholar us system

test all then wrap war into affection university

clock off terms reflecting links
like floor verse life legibly the shift safe
as ink in a just text bundles pleasure
many persons flower as fish
weaving all shape

hence
found fast at a hitch catch
the same now might if you
achieve perpetual arks under a me thing
cut off with a love cause

arking dream often is a shifting object collection
the usual rule of bring us ur fluff
to make of all the or ink way
a human bell up for making
din sort time a mind in other
we thus get with desire as the page for two
extent of affection a form of here
keeps in a certain us jam
such intention calls astounding us
ear in this all now quest jazz fits in

faces upon a naked life
playing saying mostly romance
sing on rolls the reversal

read
ink worldly moment wanderings
ink place durations on the find
colour the city to the draft
co play ask as well yell
more king knocking and furious

seek a tone beaming
ink meaning rages for truth
mighty ally a nod linked with distinct urgency
at speed the wild nod is us space
change in the moment like a whole place

nothing like a dry season of the eyes
smile that mud in the air
branching over unities
takes a person linked
all human into the confusion

turned with life diversity mimes yes
nags a scribe
one edge waking the alphabet
true anima the direction of a co here
satisfied in formal plot
complete care can obscure
concrete music hard to under lit

the echo under places made
bound in word
breathing forever ideas
ink honey it respects
sort of
a dictionary with a pulse

how the dark whispers a low song
the world diction often re fictions

wing prose of ear mode
re patterns old all
pieces out sling over being
shine other talk

just choices
place the marvellous ambition you try
loom likenessing high between us
partners curious co find coincidence
ear people sit and listen
on beyond this point

re other us with felt sound
as i ear trod settle more between
kind of vast echo on the subject
as i seek
more than fashion to free
converse in ink

with a book of the port
ask proportion
judgment close
to the edge of re change

distinct stance work draws clear in a second place
replaced will
way unfinished
stance moves of others
a favor just

ask obstacle to study collage as doubt shape
understanding no one is fie on cheer

if is pen material scratching be art
a doubt able of no compare
gives the next action

to portion time do read
ink is
to the eye a foothold
and a doubt given disclosure

to climb on
mind the other
situation now the eye
in
formation

Odyssey Poem

the legend's story
us   lashed

didn't hear the gathering

again   in eyes
is the song

Measure

re
hesitates
in
small
sums

unset
peace
writing
order
in
attention
mountain

i
almost
as
much

um
in the pulse
forms

Hunt for Optimism in the Middle Bridged

with you
is collision but if you stage
the ironic so
scribe ear
art prop
music in
off man compass
behind the invisible
i of
eros naive
would be side
strength in every epoch
faces express
i am over
ions meanwhile content is
pyknic and
portrait so my
reflection
you he is actually made of
will never place
it in terms of
facts ravelled
memory will happen browse through
ability can find then
guard
ur chance
or conversation
let us imagine that
to guard
this is the one the
only one i dedicate to you he us

<table>
<tr><td align="right">or meet in</td><td>co a</td></tr>
<tr><td align="right">person</td><td>he</td></tr>
<tr><td align="right">her</td><td>tect</td></tr>
<tr><td align="right">friend</td><td>i might be</td></tr>
<tr><td align="right">wrong</td><td></td></tr>
<tr><td align="right">in order to think</td><td>he was already</td></tr>
<tr><td align="right">ions</td><td>turned</td></tr>
<tr><td align="right"></td><td>and</td></tr>
<tr><td align="right">thirty minutes</td><td>somewhere</td></tr>
<tr><td align="right">with my</td><td></td></tr>
<tr><td align="right">reader</td><td></td></tr>
<tr><td align="right">in this</td><td>caption under the image</td></tr>
<tr><td align="right">book</td><td>staking everything</td></tr>
<tr><td align="right">changing</td><td>time</td></tr>
<tr><td align="right">art so they can convey life</td><td>the material is</td></tr>
<tr><td align="right">the</td><td></td></tr>
<tr><td align="right">landscape</td><td>t</td></tr>
<tr><td align="right">in your apartment</td><td>across from the square</td></tr>
<tr><td align="right">are</td><td>black slanting traces</td></tr>
<tr><td align="right">bring</td><td>a</td></tr>
<tr><td align="right">here i'll take a look</td><td>wild wind</td></tr>
<tr><td align="right">photograph could be</td><td>the</td></tr>
<tr><td align="right">con</td><td></td></tr>
<tr><td align="right">stopped</td><td>the bonfire</td></tr>
<tr><td align="right">antiquated</td><td>a feeling</td></tr>
<tr><td align="right"></td><td></td></tr>
<tr><td align="right">uprising</td><td>we re the</td></tr>
<tr><td align="right">i am</td><td>the</td></tr>
<tr><td align="right"></td><td>low so</td></tr>
<tr><td align="right">re</td><td>i</td></tr>
<tr><td align="right">recalled my childhood and</td><td>was sent here</td></tr>
<tr><td align="right">on</td><td></td></tr>
<tr><td align="right"></td><td>how</td></tr>
</table>

	he
skull	during the
dagger	me
i am	future political alliance
	the
guard cadets	the
sky college	was considered a
square	took him to court
red	only when she was
and the yellow	doorway, as if
division is in front of it	
the Winter Palace	the
cloak	*ta-ta*
	according to this
antic ism	the cava
supplier	near the
S	this
in	
genia	six
take	accord
in a carriage	i am not
your fifteen minutes	by Turgenev
	prop
behind one's tail	i was spring
again, didn't	a warm breeze
say	orchestral helicons
	the garden
	night
on	behind a veil of
materials	the head was
and-oil in	her chakra
a	law of genre became
elations	

ties, landscapes, and	seven
paces	it was terrifying to be
lustrated	hot she was
evidence that he ever did so	
a fighter of unequal strength he	i
the blanket	crystal
into	the
anyone	N
getting bored was	the other
getting	there was
me to see him	N
i am your father	where the key of the sullen
died	N
ness is	chakra
the ancestral throne	pal
ten based on	nine the end of
cyclopedic	
work	
corrected	i have been
which means	glass of an electric
kingdom in the	and
in the	E
ally	hand please hurry
the fifty-ninth	i
purposely took	the
ship	the
phants and forty el-	fourteen
e phants are more than enough to be happy	eight
rent from the Place	unfinished work
	ten
marched in step	chakra
let them	the occasion to
	learn

from encampment	the rice plants had
be	swamps at
	bottom
the foreign	talk
from the balconies	stick
quietly counted	spin
as they bounce against	
knees	bats
age	the King
trunks on	and someone
holding crow with	in
	i
surrounded	we didn't want to
photograph	mourning
as in a *ya*	
the copy	compels us to re
me	a re
lace of labour	
	form was quick
version of the	
semi	
wavy	
in the east	garden
towers	un
tower look like	the foreground
they travel	
the wires	thirteen
read:	what is
V	dust
protesting	pity
on	a person
from Moscow to	
D	

forever that's what a writer is like
apartment to a song
the bible god who ate the world in
narrow strips and mixed with glad
reading the
east *Ma*
i am names of
sunlight book and contents we re
read the S
gram a green
scroll with water
putting Marco Polo
out into the garden gondola
the railway workers land close
union
died metal
ships
un help of a small
pointing to the
sun one can talk
visible
flowers a re already turning
on in old age
the Venetian night climbs in with
getting old the glass
bronze behind the windows, deep down
shelf in a vast pan
room when cold
touch the bronze give
sighs and groans substance
the great cold here
reminiscing one wishes
nice the audience

the traveller   a foreign non-
death   laughing on
dead   after all they still re
in
    E
roads made   in front of
ages
curtains
N's   main action
our masts   the houses
mask   place
music stopped   the gondola
one   house walls
enchantress and regret   third floors reflected on
returned home   S
ing   s
a way   passing
back on   letting
nobody be   sacred
now the   bell rang
world is great   gray-haired
here   S
a tall   fore
in the sky   i
thundered   more
turned his back to the   innocent jokes
and left the auditorium   re
fought for this city   you must admit
the long staircase one two three four   M arc
too many steps   your book
red in a layer   but now it's late
paper   that there is no
up to the captain   about

<table>
<tr><td align="right">feet</td><td></td></tr>
<tr><td align="right">books</td><td></td></tr>
<tr><td align="right">created by a scribe’s hand</td><td>admit that</td></tr>
<tr><td align="right">vine</td><td>i have seen</td></tr>
<tr><td align="right">t</td><td>different</td></tr>
<tr><td align="right">re is such</td><td>a</td></tr>
<tr><td align="right">re</td><td>move</td></tr>
<tr><td align="right">o</td><td>we</td></tr>
<tr><td align="right">tarry</td><td>shoot from</td></tr>
<tr><td align="right">within us</td><td>the</td></tr>
<tr><td align="right">red</td><td>fist</td></tr>
<tr><td align="right">still</td><td></td></tr>
<tr><td align="right">very on about</td><td>hard</td></tr>
<tr><td align="right">roads that lead to</td><td>all</td></tr>
<tr><td align="right">our books will write on</td><td>an i less tired</td></tr>
<tr><td align="right">o</td><td>books</td></tr>
<tr><td align="right">ject the</td><td>[dot dot dot]</td></tr>
<tr><td align="right">traveller as he spoke</td><td>o</td></tr>
<tr><td align="right">ably answered   heard</td><td></td></tr>
<tr><td align="right">our</td><td></td></tr>
<tr><td align="right">listening</td><td>pressing deep</td></tr>
<tr><td align="right">telling you the same thing</td><td></td></tr>
<tr><td align="right">re neo</td><td></td></tr>
<tr><td align="right">furthers</td><td></td></tr>
<tr><td align="right">all</td><td></td></tr>
<tr><td align="right">i brought</td><td></td></tr>
<tr><td align="right">here</td><td></td></tr>
</table>

So Nets the middle of Crosby and Bleecker

signs today arm new paper
off on reading the lack as faceted present
"Goodbye Bernie!"
arg speckled night now sleeps on
silent war   if   it is dear

painting aspirations of wakeful annoyance
hands today signal
inspect each shore in brain's collage
as a break   re-trains   ears to wait

high arks in the roof of on off poems
worrying about making
worrying but not worrying about 59 cares
beat too close to buck the same

art's ear up on this room getting big
us dreams   on off   all turns
writing into a bridge
on top of others
we rethink   tall steps   in his eyes

...

strange to be
all up and ready 5:15 a.m.
a blue room sustained by emotion
angels' favorite poem
makes my eyes
Louis Sullivan
dead he is   still   an anchor

Last words from Creeley, a gain

just there here still
love thought
this day its pleasures
cared
useless not
saying what? bye and bye
city burning to be done
won't kill you twin
self wait to get out
self a thousand words
pass the end
moves on what's left
here is never done
re guard the golden
no one is none less
sound from the well
ring it a way
heard it doesn't fit?
keep looking
love even the day

Human Universe

to know more about house
not the thing's class for example
its relevance to eyed creatures
made valuable and allowed
whatever relations may overrun the earth
a way which is not divisive as no thing without plan or discipline to make
must be a way we now live in
each split is also true
order to define—prevent, deter, distract found out how to do
the act of discovering my assumption
more or less once there was
a contrary of we re able to stay
children including at least three nets in
love and flesh which seem to carry that
great if on
our way and in stone they retain the power of
a bus, as they disclose the depth mass
lure into a fire tower
the month of June fed
water into pots
to do a stew
the secret belongs in the most elementary human acts
that differ pose its old surprise
rocked by plishments

flesh is most gentle	on
flesh there is	ur bank
for all the years of	bodies
	are
one	ripened fruit
precisely	one
animal so beautiful how	content is the same juggling
show human	men are such jugglers
when the house is	equal
not exaggerated	comes to
understand	as the condition
to a restoration of human	labour
that old assertion	lit
energy and ingenuity	responding
all even	idea
man reverts to	what he does
inertia and gas	but when you have
enough of bright description	forever damn
the good	soul which softly stood
the overwhelming	real
value is	chaos generous
to fight down to it beneath the	greater crime you have allowed
we stir	sub stance which takes making the threshold
	a
	tonal place (the great
dynamic I don't know	the centre of
trouble	itself the meeting edge
of	do

go that
press it is
to touch me restore
fire immediately the speed of
actual phenomena
the result we have the ways
science has run for reason separated
like a child for example
in hopes fears faiths loves
in
responsibility to content
winds' suck of symbols increased
a word promoted
huge does make it
ear true
selective ally the particular act
selects the soother making behooves
one not to look too jauntily
on even if
lit brains function
ally can satisfy love a mystery
transpose phenomena to reality differently
reception from another
more like than different froward
act a transposition otherwise
tricky symbol maker arbitrary and willful
the stuff it works here again as nature
not isolated from content so powerful little thing
the found error will recognizes when he turns, again

a thing can be measured   self held in
motion   choose to
either way   what gets me
human being goes   disposing on entrance
you re enact it   as though we re
possess the universe as   a proof
does seek   mime will be
intent to take   and be let go
to comprehend in process   a kind you think make use of found
powers   the hieroglyphs of *Ma*
emotion we call life to   norm contradiction
act on that tremendous   possible difference
we love for its own sake   society
the equal of all transposing   re expended in the sieve net words become
when it proceeds   like natures past
from the threshold through and back again with   knowledge on
quality) to text a world here   bearable
being several   in human memory bled out in the hands of
hidden generalization   monsters people are to
break the full circuit of   knowing how to
act any point meeting edge of the world   to pass over
here we re experience   the purpose
fresh coming fresh   work a concrete thing
going does that inside house more   as danger
acute at the door is   apt to reason ultimate arts
influence reality   us arts in chance
ears   every energy can be we
human   universe

Twombly > Chicago > NY

as urban as
a whale
who conserves
generates

ur
cement

cooling
the hot
cause
and us

a wish
show we
here are
meeting

sand
or
ampersand

what aids the act of
teaches
the year

Language & Architecture

act articulate avoid annoy
bustle burgle bully browse brag
correct calm coax
disguise dwindle delight

Architecture & Language

embed epitomize estrange exhume
figure flummox flatter fork fix
gesture gamble glam glom gerrymander

Language & Architecture

hallow herd hide heed
involve ignite idolize ignore
jubilate jinx juggle join
kindle keep kiss kill

Architecture & Language

loom lobby lather liken
mine mend mourn mystify meander
normalize nationalize nudge need

Language & Architecture

officiate opacify ostracize overdo
persist placate perplex probe
quarry quilt quibble queue
rouse rehearse rank ramble reveal
sleep slur stipulate situate surmise

Architecture & Language

tickle topple temper transform
urge unite usher understate undo
vacillate veil vex vow

Language & Architecture

waffle wizen wake whip warp woof
x-rate xeno-philanthropize

Architecture & Language

yield yoke yearn yawn
zip zonk zenith zero

WORDpark
is a place for
shifting into
another mode
of transport.
Reading
and writing, writing
and reading, make ways
much wider than streets can.
Do we need to spell it out?
No not really. Not really.
What it means is what it does. What it does is what it means.
When you stop long enough to ask scribbling and quibbling
what is it all about this time
where have they come from
where are they going these
words here there everywhere
when on other days there are only cars cars cars trucks and s.u.v.s?
No no nonsense: Honk Honk Honk! It is not the mind but the engine
idling guzzling time gas space while the human race hell even dogs
would if they could say hey "It just does not *woof* have to be this way."
No it does not have to. We
can say what the sidewalk says morning noon and night it says even
even the sidewalk says Write on
Write the city free With chalk?
Go for a walk! while you we
talk this is not the Yes it is
but this is not the place to
balk Pick it up the pencil
pick it up the pen let the ink run run and do not stop till the silence
is a friendly one and
the parking meters
have all changed
into fruit trees
carved by lovers
dog lovers or you know
utopians utopians
with dictionaries
and hutzpah.

Arch of Enjoyment

now gives way to larger need
now to ur if
space of enjoyment

it will not sever roughly
from matters we have taken carefully

filtered by fun to function
in line with line we find
a city within
words

pleasant almost

where the social oval
invented the geo
option the re artly
co slam example
the ear
ur rounded by the vast park
intended to archi a succession of rooms
hallway and vestibule
half an acre pools together
paraphernalia for word rooms
each the caldarium
ear to be stadium

or we say a mosaic fountain
painting with din a room art park
where meet and talk a public we made
making us
offer enjoyment

yes
perhaps paces about them
they were in a sense
the place
prepared itself for sensual
text
may already co in this

they themselves approach ero
architecture polymorpho
valent art

here is an art
ur re built under the centuries
these were collective works

poets
human sculptors
who were familiar with meanings and scenes
play a primal architecture
by the act of love
together with all the refinements
diaphanous movement of the world music
times' matron sometimes the mistress
of dizzying images
responded with omni
standing

us
in the hand of space
seated on sleep
is it not an example of an art
archi

where a space of sensuality should be
looking for it

present
tended in contact
acts in a setting
carved into the sensual profusion
disappear beneath that pleasure

animals joy and love the path to through
it was able to make
beings re ecstasy an ecstasy
the flesh but an absolute art
silent about this
beautiful more or less us ecstasy
on their faces
cosmic as a sphere
forms make love with the same joy work

the here space is limited
by the body of the other
text
merely to impart this truth
the city
architecture serves
situated within
occupies that text we re posit
its owner
built texture
an archi archi
directed toward a swell typo

between urban and rural
archi ification does get us
susceptible existence
either it results from building influence
or over a slender margin
blished to span according to a pre
and so on

architecture plays
by being urb ject to a sting plan
spontaneous

it is this that makes the distant
near appear
its influence takes place
here

to abolish all forms of the former
re dominant force
of the city in uniform
success
require diversity double
a city in the city

often inspired by myth topia
building an entire city
utopia as cosmological consideration
into the urban core
domination
being transposed in ink
as more

city is read
in spatial practice
pace of habit
multi fun
by others in search
can speak
an archi enjoyment
ready based on a vague fun
these archi considerations lead us
to the city as
an archi wish to will
revolutionary arts

forgotten in the construct
constructed for you
that
will be offered part of you
will be able to
erase

scribes over inkers
dancing a building of here art
we ask dance more from the arch house of pleasure
a gentle shore
excited the artery
the flash of charming archi
ably began to build
philosophy
sensate
world for a graduated flame

loud
we are not far here
from the similar

building
a pleasure for the work of passions
into the record of question
discoveries
to the depths of connection

between
does not in any way resemble
one of our buildings
establish a great experiment only
or a pal

some difficult society must differ vastly
families having verse gain ground

archi ification
peri ification
the multi-ordial external internal synth alog
places
the other world starting
from the point of archi
marked by actical fun
internal on the other
laws of fun

archi ification
would be the surprising
laden with space of enjoyment
enjoyment
not entirely convincing
ledge space of the pan
yet
responding to between

clearly different
taken to be the analog
can differ and yet
correspond

an upright stone
part whole
designates the analog
partially apparently
similar
logy with metaphor
stood as
archi
we

discover
magic the wide range of
contact
communicates contiguity syntagmatically
by contra mime paradigm

mediation
a time to heal

touching magic
by contact
with analogy

participating in life or play
toward the world
recounts a different drama

the sting
operating within
archi mime

up ending
enables the archi base
is
co ur alog do
i
din

Systematic Encounter (in Plural Parts)

2. The Plan

2b. The Plan, revised for Epimetheus

2c. Hephaestean Paradigm

∞

^

~ | **Ho** | > ∞ < | **Ho** | ~

~ | **Di** | > ∞ (…) ∞ < | **De** | ~

~ | **Di** | > ∞ < | **De** | ~

~ | **Ho** | > ∞ (…) ∞ < | **De** | ~

~ | **Kr** | > ∞ < | **Kr** | ~

~ | **Di** | > ∞ (…) ∞ < | **Kr** | ~

~ | **De** | > ^ ^ ^ < | **De** | ~

∞ < **Di** **Ho** **Kr** < ∞

— — —

~ ~ ~

2d. Off-Cut Frivolities for Future Understudy Mask Distribution

Ho – (lop): lger ~ [namesake linguist]	Ho – rizon entangler
Di – (lop): l ~ [pickled pepper]	Di – lemma dissector
De – (lop): rek ~ [iced airport]	De – isosceles scraper
Kr – (lop): isjanis ~ [is Janus]	Kr – inkle invector

Ho-Di,
Ho-Ho,
Di-Di,
De-Di,
Di-Di,
De-Di,
Ho-Di,
De-Ho,
Kr-Di,
Kr-Kr,
Di-Di,
Kr-Di,
De-Di,
De-De,
namesake linguist

Ho-Ho,
Ho-Di,
Di-Ho,
De-Di,
Di-Ho,
De-Di,
Ho-Ho,
De-Di,
Kr-Ho,
Kr-Di,
Di-Ho,
Kr-Di,
De-Ho,
De-Di,
pickled alloglyph

Ho-Kr,
Ho-Ho,
Di-Kr,
De-Ho,
Di-Kr,
De-Ho,
Ho-Kr,
De-Ho,
Kr-Kr,
Kr-Ho,
Di-Kr,
Kr-Ho,
De-Kr,
De-Ho,
isosceles airport

Ho-Ho,
Ho-Kr,
Di-De,
De-Kr,
Di-De,
De-Kr,
Ho-De,
De-Kr,
Kr-Kr,
Kr-Kr,
Di-Kr,
Kr-Kr,
De-De,
De-Kr,
Janus threshold

Hephaestus, laughed at by gods

The far fallen smith
returns from his troubled hearth
to save the cosmic day

Caught up as it is
all glaring
in blaze of brazen truth

Even out of season
he finds a quenching way

Soothing strife
by limp and pour
of fabricated life

Poe—inciples Concentrate

In speaking of the poetic contradiction in terms

I need scarcely observe in effect and in fact no longer such

There are no doubt many who precisely the fact

In regard to the Iliad we popular again

That the extent of a poetical not be essentially damaged as truths

On the other hand it is whistled down the wind

A remarkable instance will break at last

Very few perhaps are a southern midsummer night

One of the finest cursed a way

In this composition we other works of this author

While the epi poems sake

With as deep waters of poetry and truth

Dividing the world of mind in a word to beauty

An immortal instinct deep with brief and indeterminate glimpses

The struggle to apprehend and to feel as poetic

The poetic sent ecting them as poems

To recapitulate the whatever either with duty or with truth

A few words however the atmosphere and the real essence of the poem

I cannot better introduce and as silently steal away

With no great range ping beauty in the wax-works

Among the minor poems is living voice

The rhythmical flow here sembles the rain

The taint of which I speak is a name

It was the mis earnestness with which they are uttered

It is by no means my design or his reward

Now this fable answers its altogether

Among the melodies *ish* there too

It has been the fashion to remember them

One of the noblest—and speaking has broken many more

The haunted ur

The vigour of this thesis of the poem

Among the minor peaks to my spirit of thee

Although the rhythm love of woman

From days that are no more

Thus although in a very cursory and imperfect harmony manifest

We shall reach however more immediate vine majesty—of her love

Let me conclude *to fight and hero-like to die*

Lamp of Beauty

in the outset of organic nature is avid pursuit

will a direct imitation of the acanthus leaf

Again the Romanesque arch is beau selves wreathe them in capitals

Now would insist where the one is ordinary be the other

The first so-called ornament then is arrangement less perceived

in association with an oval placed in a hollow

will evidently follow crags and ex processes of crystallization

I have just convicted every place in which lines are necessary

The ornament whose cause forms the stones of it

In the same clause must not multiply a King's arms

also follow you are an architect not a writing master

Inscriptions appear so times form which is not nor ever can be

all this want of organization followed the dances of angels

Thus tread drapery is indeed noble base

Closely connected with the abuse of scrolls beautifully placed

No I do not mean pegs and hats upon them

One of the worst enemies some likelihood of its dropping off

I might proceed but the task is serious convictions to dice

Thus far of what is fair on the bronze of Ghiberti

very being imitative form

the place for bodily press on thought

Now let us consider instant colour forever

Apply this press on thought before it will revive

Hence a genera as moths to a candle

will be much removed also

Another strange smith at his anvil

not lost in the general press of emptiness

Must not beauty with the calm of pastoral solitude

Thus far then of the place sink into ingenious carving

portion so much transgressing the very simplest of ties

the first guess the real intention builds

This rule applies to the roll two subordinates

if possible enter into details the tower of Pisa

One principle of Proportion to name secondary joints

The leaf of this plant has five ribs unique they are not

The other archi wherein danger consists in dignity

I have said that to the severest mouldings

Now observe in the whole subject of abstraction

Happy opinion vanishes into perfect sculpture

Nearness to the eye however is not stripped of a single plume

Under these limitations think architecture of the world

Our final inquiry to be for other causes expedient

First think in making groups of things

broad conclusion we marble and so leave them

dependence being secure spots on them

should be colours of a piece of opal I conclude enough refined

Restraining selves may express Organic form rent with their forms

Or form sub current with forms Organic tract

ground of another Organ forms entirely the most vivid colour

the opposite side of Venice Pure archi on the left

intense love carved marble the curse of noble characters

Consider red stone These characteristics wing the sheep

If Tower

if
often
lun
ched
in
the
tower
only
place
to see
& not
blind
point o
f center
seems to
limit pow
er turn wh
en we visit
dynamic me
asure stances
search orologic
seem remingled
imagination a first
paradox to make it
metaphor a zero you
can visit the *Hunch* a bird's eye
table our topography struggles
in a sense that is to make me
mory a Paris you pace in ugh's
monument forms up to its opposition of
the present world and me into a living
being situated a little apart from witness
fixes historical and social is performed also
an initiation a riddle to enter here we reinvoke
the cohort of internal meanders ear lacework ification
as in a face usly illuminated insinuate delectable reality as
a familiar little world as on an ocean dreaming one can feel a world

Roland's Tower, X'd

Maupassant restaurant
in contest able
to touch at
writing these lines
A made

somehow or
mythic function is to join
again earth
ally empty sign is
dialect era

singular either
history with
who can
tomorrow but the
notion jet

d'art Tower
his Tower in
it
quite naturally touches
undoubtedly the last story

of a
Tower should be
in
it re conquered

elementary to

explore one
it adds to
harmony
the city joins up with
major hand

the chapter *Notre*
us to transcend
Hence
a list mode
offers exposed

intelligence but a
scrim of
real
space in which
not is also to

mask a net
the pan or a
leap out to
that
second is the

Middle as the
made now certain
vision
within space

the horizon stacked one

after the functions
war hereby participating
makes every
situated a little
doubt a very old Tower still allows

us however
being mobilized
ject
with exploration
what defines its open

structure how
enormity does astonish
metal pillars
insofar as it gives
tiny square object

Furnish into it
sentiment hence
exudes
as well as
it is an instance to the

ancient American
pleasures essential
panorama can
function understand the
world and world?

Notes on Poems & Sources

Many of the poems gathered here respond to sources I've learned from through an exploratory process midway between reading and writing, finding and making, un-making and re-making. Seeking the common (and uncommon) grounds where the architecture of poetry & the poetry of architecture meet, this experiment—although largely improvisatory—has been shaped by rules I've found, adapted, broken or bent along the way to *archi-poetry*. In ancient Greek, such sources, rules and aims were called *archai*; while *poïesis* meant "making" anything needed or desired.

The following notes acknowledge a growing archive of *archi-poetry* sources and resources:

"Agog" is an opening micro-rejoinder to Christian Bök's "The Xenagogue"—the middle-most poem in *The Xenotext* (Coach House Books, 2015). "Xeno-Laps" leap across choice page-gaps in the midst of the same strangely boundless book.

"How Speak", "Inauguries" and "Language & Architecture" were first published in *Quality Out of Control: Standards for Measuring Architecture* (Routledge, 2010).

"Sticks & Stones, a reWorlding" rejigs George Bowering's poem "Wattle" in *Sticks & Stones* (Talon Books, 1989).

"Fly-Trap Test" was inspired by three sources: Robert Musil's short essay "Flypaper" (featuring a sticky, letter size sheet, made in Canada) in *Posthumous Papers of a Living Author* (Eridanos Press, 1987); Lucian of Samosata's encomium to "The Fly" [ca170 CE] in *The Works of Lucian, Vol. 3* (Clarendon Press, 1905); and Charles Simic's poem "The Story" in *Return to a Place Lit by a Glass of Milk* (Braziller, 1974).

"So Nets a beginning" takes a vertical section cut through the first six of Ted Berrigan's *Sonnets* [1964] (Penguin, 2000); "So Nets the middle of Crosby & Bleecker" slices through sonnets #42-45, #80. In my view, traces of Louis Sullivan's Bayard-Condict Building (at the corner of Crosby and Bleecker in NYC) are woven throughout Berrigan's *Sonnets*.

"Aristotle's Nik, fragments" are excerpts from a longer poem reinterpreting Book 6 of Aristotle's *Nicomachean Ethics* (Oxford, 1998)—primary source for the architecture of the mean.

"Art History (with Hiccups)" echoes a mix of sources: "Oral History (with Hiccups)" in *The Collected Stories of Lydia Davis* (Farrar, Straus and Giroux, 2009); Pliny the Elder's *Natural History* (XXXV: 15, 43), as cited in Victor Stoichita *A Short History of the Shadow* (Reaktion, 1997); and Aristophanes' speech in Plato's *Symposium* (188e-193e).

"Roland the Para-Tower", "If Tower" and "Roland's Tower, X'd" recycle Roland Barthes' title essay in *The Eiffel Tower* [1964] *and Other Mythologies* (Farrar, Straus and Giroux, 1979).

"Ark Fundations, Roving Renovations (8 Beams)" are excerpts from a longer series ripping down Ronald Johnson's *Ark: The Foundations* (North Point Press, 1980).

"Orgy of Cities", "Measure", "Time Materials", and "Odyssey Poem" recast four poems by Robert Hass: respectively, "The Origin of Cities" in *Praise* (Ecco Press, 1979); "Measure" in *Field Guild* (Yale University Press, 1973); "Time and Materials" and "Envy of Other People's Poems" in *Time and Materials* (Ecco Press, 2007).

"Age of Huts, Midway Para-Cuts" one-up jump-cuts "The Chinese Notebook" in Ron Silliman *Age of Huts (compleat)* (University of California Press, 2007); "Halfabet: words leaping Manifest No" reinvents the juncture of "Manifest" and "Non"—the middle poems in Silliman's *The Alphabet* (University of Alabama Press, 2008).

"Tunnelling Through" first appeared in *On Site review* #53 "Geology" (Spring 2013) p53.

"Writing an Aid to Me" threads short-cuts through the labyrinth of Lyn Hejinian's *Writing is an Aid to Memory* (Sun & Moon Press, 1996).

"Hunt for Optimism in the Middle Bridged" revamps "The Middle of the Book or Thereabouts" in Viktor Shklovsky 's [1933] experimental novel *A Hunt for Optimism* (Dalkey Archive, 2012). A companion piece appears in *On Site review* #34 "On Writing" (Spring 2016).

"Last Words from Creeley, a gain" recycles terminal clippings from Robert Creeley *On Earth: Last Poems and an Essay* (University of California Press, 2006).

"Human Universe" makes a poem from the eponymous [1951] essay in *Collected Prose: Charles Olson* (University of California Press, 1997); "Twombly>Chicago>NY" reimagines "For Cy Twombly Faced with His First Chicago & N.Y. Shows" in *The Collected Poems of Charles Olson* (University of California Press, 1987).

"WORDpark" was part of an urban intervention, and photo-essay, first published in *On Site review* #30: "Ethics and Publics" (Fall 2013).

"Arch of Enjoyment" makes poetry from Henri Lefebvre's essay "Architecture" in *Toward an Architecture of Enjoyment* (University of Minnesota Press, 2014). This poem first appeared in *The American Society for Aesthetics Newsletter* v35 n2 (Summer 2015).

"Systematic Encounter (in Plural Parts)" is a set of ekphrastic poems responding to a painting exhibition called *Re-Configuring Abstraction*, School of Art Gallery, University of Manitoba (2012).

"Hephaestus, laughed at by gods" recalls an archi-poetic scene in the *Iliad* (1.570-611).

"Poe—inciples Concentrate" tightens the chains of Poe's manifesto "The Poetic Principles" [ca1849] in *The Complete Works of Edgar Allan Poe* (Tally Hall Press, 1974).

"Lamp of Beauty" radically foreshortens the middle chapter of John Ruskin's *Seven Lamps of Architecture* [1849] (Wiley & Sons, 1877).

Acknowledgements

I am immensely grateful to Arthur Schaller and Richard Virr for enabling this project to take root in the exceptionally transformative circumstances they allowed me to infiltrate, roughly a decade ago, when my curious quest for archi-poetry happily resumed. Thanks to everyone I've encountered in Winnipeg's thriving poetry community for their idiosyncratic company and tolerant bemusement. Colin Smith, Marjorie Poor, Jan Horner, and many others, have nudged me along in manifold ways. I've benefited from numerous workshops led by poets who've conspired to keep my experimental ponderings playful, especially Méira Cook, Jennifer Still, and Steven Ross Smith; and wish to acknowledge the local institutions providing a place for poetry to emerge. In no particular order, these include the Manitoba Writers' Guild, the Writers' Collective, the Millennium Public Library (host of Speaking Crow), and the University of Manitoba's Centre for Creative Writing and Oral Culture.

I am indebted to Garry Thomas Morse, poetry editor at Signature Editions, for enabling this book to happen, and all the various editors who have bravely published my work. Of these I especially like to thank Clarise Foster (*CV2*), Stephanie White (*On Site review*), and David Greenblatt (American Society for Aesthetics). Lastly, I wish to thank Lisa Landrum, my collaborator in love and life, for her courageous creativity, wisdom and support.

About the Author

Ted Landrum is a poet, critic, teacher, and artist, with extensive architectural and teaching experience in the US and Canada. He began writing what he calls "archi-poetry" while studying architecture at Ball State University in Indiana. He continued writing and performing poetry while practicing architecture in New York City, being influenced by the jazz, the theatre, and the tumult of that great metropolis. Having lived in nearly a dozen cities, from Chicago to Montreal, Ottawa to Vermont, Ted now lives in Winnipeg, where he teaches architecture at the University of Manitoba. His poetry and criticism have been published in a wide variety of venues: *On Site Review, Brooklyn Rail, Lemon Hound, CV2, The American Society for Aesthetics, The Winnipeg Review, Edge Condition,* and in two books by Routledge: *Quality Out of Control,* and *Confabulations: Storytelling in Architecture*. Between distractions, he is building an archive of archi-poetry research at www.ubuloca.com

Eco-Audit

Printing this book using Rolland Enviro 100 Book instead of virgin fibres paper saved the following resources:

Trees	Solid Waste	Water	Air Emissions
1	23 kg	1,853 L	208 kg